P9-AQA-611

AMEDEO   MODIGLIANI
1884 - 1920

Loan Exhibition

AMEDEO MODIGLIANI

OCTOBER 14 - NOVEMBER 13
1971

For the Benefit of the Museum of Modern Art, New York

ACQUAVELLA GALLERIES, INC.
18 East 79th Street, New York

Copyright © Acquavella Galleries, Inc., 1971
Library of Congress Catalogue Card Number: 73-168570

Acknowledgments

This exhibition would not have been possible without the unstinting coope-ration of many public museums and private collectors. On behalf of the Acquavella Galleries, Inc., I would like to express our deep gratitude to all the lenders for their graciousness in sharing their masterpieces with the general public, and to Dr. Alfred Werner for his assistance in preparing this catalogue.

Nicholas M. Acquavella

LENDERS TO THE EXHIBITION

Albright-Knox Art Gallery, Buffalo, New York
The Evergreen House, Baltimore
The Solomon R. Guggenheim, Museum New York
The Indianapolis Museum of Art, Indianapolis
The Los Angeles County Museum of Art, Los Angeles
The Marion Koogler McNay Art Institute, San Antonio, Texas
The Metropolitan Museum of Art, New York
The Museum of Modern Art, New York
The Phillips Collection, Washington, D. C.

The Harry N. Abrams Family Collection
Mr. and Mrs. James W. Alsdorf
Mr. and Mrs. Arnold Askin
Mr. and Mrs. Keith Barish
Mr. and Mrs. John A. Beck
Mr. Ernst Beyeler
Mr. Edward A. Bragaline
Mr. Nathan Cummings
Mr. Joseph H. Hazen
The Alex Hillman Family Foundation
The Freddy and Regina T. Homburger Collection
Mr. R. Sturgis Ingersoll
Mr. and Mrs. Simon Jaglom
Katherine and the Late Adolphe A. Juviler
Mr. and Mrs. Alexander Lewyt
Mr. and Mrs. Robert J. Newman
Mr. and Mrs. Henry Pearlman
Mr. and Mrs. Klaus G. Perls
Mr. and Mrs. Gustave Ring
The Ritter Foundation, Inc.
Mr. Leo M. Rogers
Mr. and Mrs. Paul Sampliner
Mrs. Evelyn Sharp
Paul and Odette Wurzburger
Mr. Richard S. Zeisler
and Anonymous Private Collectors

THE ETERNAL MODIGLIANI

By Alfred Werner

> « *The art of Modigliani is not accessible imme-
> diately to all. To approach it one must enter it
> deeply, enter it even with an effort. Then this
> work grows with a grandeur and with a purity
> that comes from laws the most secret and eternal
> of the art of all ages* ».
>
> Arthur Pfannstiel (1929)

I

ach of us, rereading any of the numerous straight biographies or the more romantic novels dealing with Amedeo Modigliani (1884-1920) that have proliferated in the past half century, must feel as though trapped in a theatre where a well-known classical tragedy is being played. The end is inevitable, the charming hero must die prematurely and yet we would like to step in and halt the performance - no, he must not be allowed to perish wretchedly, he must round out his life, for his pleasure and for the benefit of humanity, eager to receive all that his genius might create.....

Does Modigliani's life stand in the way of a cool, detached, critical appreciation of his work? « The pale, dark-haired Bohemian sitting on the *terrasse* of the Café de la Rotonde or the Dome, a glass of absinthe before him, drawing likenesses of patrons in sharp, rapid strokes, and graciously offering them to would-be customers for a few francs each, or even for a drink.....».

La vie passionnée de Modigliani was considered dramatic enough to serve as the subject of a French film. This movie presented the artist as a ranting and misbehaving hippie who, astonishingly, somehow managed to produce a number of fine pictures. A different view was taken by Maud Dale, wife of the noted New York collector Chester Dale, when she wrote about Modigliani in 1929. The artist had been dead for less than a decade, yet his « legend », or rather « legends », had already buried the truth. She saw him not as a man of flesh and blood, but as a puppet, a pathetic Pagliaccio who « encountered, in the many adventures that befell him, so great a suffering that he died of it ».

One of those responsible for the diffusion, in the Anglo-Saxon world of the more common, more delicate notion of Modigliani as a « painter under a curse » was Charles Douglas who, like Mrs. Dale, had never met the artist, but tried to reconstruct his life on the strength of what he was told by a variety of « Montparnos ». Due to concoctions like his *Artist Quarter,* some people still think of artists as being mainly drug addicts, alcoholics and sex maniacs rather than as creators who, whatever frivolities they may engage in during their leisure time, devote the better part of their lives to serious work.

On the other hand, the artist's daughter Jeanne, though still a baby when he died, was reared by his family and had sources of information unavailable to others when writing her *Modigliani senza leggenda*. She did not endeavor to « whitewash » her father. Alcohol and drugs may have been necessary to the frail, unsuccessful and unappreciated foreigner from a small town, suffering from shyness and frustration in the overwhelming and overpowering French capital, but as she points out, these stimulants neither produced nor even released his genius. If the painter committed certain nuisance when drunk, it must be borne in mind that an artist's occasional brief outbursts of necessity get more attention than the long quiet periods of labor preceding them. Debunking the « romantic legend of a death due to hunger, alcohol and Heaven knows what metaphysical torments », Jeanne put the blame squarely on the tuberculosis from which her father suffered all his life.

One point that Modigliani's biographers do not always seem to stress sufficiently is that his extravagances were not important enough to prevent some outstanding men and women from recognizing his true values as a rare person. He had, in different degrees, the friendship or at least attention of such fellow artists as Leon Bakst, Constantin Brancusi, Juan Gris, Moise Kisling, Jacques Lipchitz, Pablo Picasso, Diego Rivera, Chaim Soutine, Maurice Vlaminck and Ossip Zadkine, and of such intellectuals as the poets Blaise Cendrars, Jean Cocteau, and Max Jacob. Nearly all of these, incidentally, sat for him. Vlaminck, who was very choosy about his friendships, wrote about Modigliani: « I knew him when he was hungry. I have seen him drunk. But in no instance did I ever find him lacking in nobility or generosity. I never knew him to be guilty of the least baseness, although I have seen him irascible at having to admit to the power of money, which he scorned but which could so hamper him and hurt his pride ». And the sculptor Zadkine described him as « a young god masquerading as a workman in his Sunday best » (he failed to add that this « Sunday best » consisted of a corduroy suit, checked shirt and red belt that Modigliani wore every day).

Another point that should have occupied all his biographers - and did the wiser ones - was the astonishing phenomenon that when the artist was most beset by disappointment and sickness, he managed to produce canvases unmatched in balance, harmony and pensive aristocratic detachment. Artists somehow do not always fit preconceived notions, as far as the character of their work is concerned. For if art were a simple reflection of biographical facts, one would expect of Modigliani torrents of orgiastic color, untidily smeared onto the canvas in thick impasto. Yet, even if he did not have the strength to resist alcohol, he was able to dedicate himself to the most complete and perfect aesthetic transfiguration of his inner imagery. With this strange phenomenon in mind, Claude Roy suggested that a biographer, who had to write about the master on the strength of the extant pictures alone, without any other evidence, might conclude that the creator of these serene paintings must have led a quiet, sheltered life.

Possibly, despite all vicissitudes - which even his solicitous daughter cannot deny - Modigliani's fourteen years in Paris were not as unhappy as an ordinary citizen would think. He was really frustrated only to the extent that, at one point poor health and lack of funds required him to give up sculpture, to which he would have liked to dedicate himself to the exclusion of everything else (fortunately, what he learned in concentrating on sculpture was not wasted, and it clearly enhanced the formal strength and solidity of his painting). Beethoven, deaf and isolated, wrote that only the artist or the scholar carried his happiness within him. In the same spirit, Rodin believed that true artists were almost the only men doing their work with pleasure. Nor can it be doubted that in a career stretching over no more than a decade and a half, Modigliani accomplished what is a creative man's highest goal: to forge a vocabulary, a language entirely his own, an expression satisfactory to his needs.

Possibly, then, our artist, as a truly creative person, suffered less during his short, hectic life than many a bourgeois with a secure job. This was, at any rate, the opinion of Michel-Georges Michel, who knew Modigliani personally and refused to shed tears over the fate of « poor Modi ». In his novel, *Les Montparnos*, Modrulleau (i.e. Modigliani) protests to the doctor who approaches him for drinking too much:

> « I need a flame in order to paint, in order to be consumed by fire. My *concierge* and the butcher boy have no need for alcohol, especially if it does them harm. They must conserve their precious lives ... So what difference does it make if I give an instant of

my life, if in exchange I can create a work that, perhaps, will last »?

The essence of Modigliani - the burning desire to create and to seek fulfillment and happiness in creation - is reflected in these lines (which may record what Modigliani actually said to the writer).

Nonetheless, the sensation of deep-seated pity, mingled with anger over our inability to avert catastrophe, seizes us whenever we come across the works of artists, from Masaccio to Wols, who unexpectedly passed away *nel mezzo del cammin di nostra vita,* «midway in the journey of our life», as Modigliani's compatriot and favorite poet, Dante, had sung. Why did not mankind possess, during Modigliani's lifetime, the means to control tuberculosis? And why were there so few to recognize his importance and to buy his pictures? Why was he - and, let us not forget, his loyal companion Jeanne Hébuterne as well - not permitted an existence less troubled by financial worries, malnutrition, poor housing and, above all, the nearabsence of that life of fame which, for the artist, is the only real life?

Had we been in Paris at the time of his struggles, in all likelihood we would not have appreciated his efforts, steeped as we would have been in the traditions of the Ecole des Beaux-Arts, and hence, in a diluted version of High Renaissance aesthetics. There is also something bitterly ironic about the fact that Modigliani, who, as an untidy and unruly drunk, had received more attention from police officers than from the Art Establishment, was given a hero's funeral at the Pere Lachaise cemetery. There is pity - and admiration. For from his feverish, frail body and from his drug and alcoholic-stimulated mind, Modigliani produced paintings and drawings on a par with those of his happier, more successful colleagues, especially the solid, professorial Matisse and the sharp-witted, calculating Picasso. It is, perhaps, a miracle that he even managed to live to be thirty-five, and that his work exudes a melancholy grace not to be found elsewhere, a refinement, a subtlety that is perfect, completely devoid of incrustrations of dross.

I I

It has been suggested that Modigliani had exhausted his spiritual and intellectual resources by the day - January 24, 1920 - he drew his last breath in the Hospital de la Charite. A German term describes euphemistically those who, in the relatively brief span of time allotted to them, reached their peak of perfection. Was Modigliani one of those « Fruhvollendete »? To judge by the surviving work - more than four hundred oils, an uncounted number of drawings, watercolors and gouaches, and more than twenty stone carvings - he was always in the ascendancy. Even in the paintings he created in his final months - such as the one of the pregnant Jeanne Hébuterne in a chemise, or in his only self-portrait - there is not the slightest indication of a dwindling *élan vital,* a lessening will-to-form, though the body weakened by a combination of alcoholism and overwork was approaching disintegration.

It is, perhaps, idle to speculate whether Modigliani might have continued to paint in the style that now makes his pictures easily identified by a layman. In all likelihood, he would have gone on creating « Modiglianis », had he been allowed an additional decade or two. But we would have been spared something like the spectacle of his dull-witted drinking companion, Maurice Utrillo, whose work grew feebler and feebler. On the contrary, with increasing maturity, coupled with greater emotional security, these putative post-1920 Modiglianis might have been even more refined than the earlier ones - if that be possible - just as a violinist, after years of practice, eliminates the last vestiges of uncouthness and crudeness in tone, to extract from his instrument pure sounds whose very existence he could not have imagined in the awkwardness of his youth.

There would not have been any surprises, though. Between 1905 and 1920, Picasso developed a dozen different styles, and a layman can be forgiven if he finds it hard to understand that *The Harlequin's Family, Les Demoiselles d'Avignon, Portrait of Kahnweiler, Vive la France, Madame Picasso* and *Pierrot Seated* are by one and the same artist. Morever, Modigliani was less precocious than the Spaniard, who was an accomplished painter by the time he was fourteen, The Italian, three years Picasso's junior, did not reveal any premature genius of this sort.

For a while he was under the influence of his first teacher, Guglielmo Michele, in whose studio at Livorno he worked between 1899 and 1900. This can be gathered from the few surviving pre-1906 pictures. Michele, an landscapist, had been a student of Giovanni Fattori, a representative of the Macchiaioli, a Tuscan group who used the *macchia* (dash of color) in painting pleasant villages, country roads and the radiance of the sun on earth and water in an idiom only vaguely related to that of the

Impressionists. But Modigliani never developed any strong taste for landscape. Nor did the taste of his teachers at the academies of Florence and Venice seem to have had any lasting influence upon him, though it is conceivable that they helped him foster his talent as a draughtsman.

Indeed, his stupendous draughtsmanship was appreciated long before his accomplishments as a painter. His remarkable indifference to the very anatomical data that the academies held sacred must not lead us to overlook his ability to follow the strictest conventions. He could break the rules because he knew them (like Gino Severini, he believed that « to distort is to correct nature in terms of the artist's sensibility »). The best summation of the importance of this segment of his work is by Claude Roy, who wrote:

> « If some cataclysm had deprived the world of all Modigliani's paintings and spared the drawings, the latter would certainly have secured him a place in the front rank as a superb interpreter of human bodies and faces ... Modigliani is one of the supremely gifted few who seem to say everything with next to nothing; in whose works a simple line, a brief allusion, a faintly indicated gesture suffice to bring before us the infinite, incredible profusion of human life ».

As a painter, Modigliani seems to have tried to break away from what might be described as a post-Macchiaioli manner even when he was an art student in Venice. But it was only as an independent - and soon indigent - artist on Montmartre that he began to grope, successfully, for a style of his own (despite all traces of « influence »). The portraits done between 1906 and 1914 - and « portraits » of one sort or another were virtually all that the single-minded master was to produce - reveal the impact of Toulouse-Lautrec. One can also find affinities to the turbulent early work of Rouault. From Cézanne, Modigliani learned to build with broad planes and large areas of color, and also to « distort », to deviate from reality to achieve aesthetic beauty or to heighten emotional pitch. In his pocket he carried a reproduction of *Boy in a Red Vest* which he would pull out at the mention of Cézanne; he would hold it up to his face like a breviary, draw it to his lips and kiss it. He also had high regard for Picasso (his own works were, for a while, reminiscent of the melancholy Blue Period pictures). Summoned to paint the portrait of a collector, Modigliani spotted a work by the Spaniard in the apartment; he begged the owner to keep it nearby while he was painting, as an example and an inspiration.

Every young man needs guides, even idols, on his road to self-fulfillment. What is remarkable about these early works is that, though they are not the « typical » Modiglianis that turn up in the master's final five or six years, they are, nonetheless, quite strong. They have none of the sweetness and slickness of academic portraits of *La Belle Epoque.* The thick black outlines, the vigorously accentuated red lips and the unruly brushwork are reminiscent of the creations by German Expressionists, though any direct influence is most unlikely. With their vehement striving for expression, their feverish unrest, these pictures have the haunting quality that we find in El Greco. They are not mere exercises in painterly craftsmanship. Young Modigliani already appears as a searcher for character who concentrates on the essentials of face and hands, giving only summary treatment to the sitter's torso.

Indeed, Modigliani was a first-rate psychologist. He retained his interest in characterization even when, later on, his concessions to « Realism » became fewer, and less and less marked. After all, he never went as far in decomposing reality as did the Cubist painters, whose sitters almost disappear in a maze of fragmented detail. Admittedly, the geometric simplification in the work of the « mature » Modigliani is as « unnaturalistic » as the color he often gives to hair or skin, without regard for the actual hue. Yet the delft pattern-maker never omitted a sitter's personality. This trait is, of course, not always noted by the hurried gallery-goer. His quick glance grasps only the superficial aspects by which anyone believes he can spot a typical Modigliani from a distance of a hundred feet:

The frontal pose; the sitter's S-shape; the flat, mask-like face; the almond eyes; the spatulate or slightly twisted nose; the pursed, small mouth; the head thinned out to the extreme; the neck either over-long or virtually non-existent; the calculated disproportion between head, torso and legs; the sculptural approach (maintained despite the artist's total indifference to modeling, light and atmosphere); and, finally, the resonant and intensely luminous, yet uncomplicated color applied with an accuracy that is absent in the majority of pictures by the masters to whom he is often linked by historians - the Expressionists.

III

« Modigliani, as an artist, was a witness; he did not open a new
way of pictorial expression, except for himself; he did not revolu-
tionize the poetic vision of the world, but offered it one that
was both secret and touching. Like Soutine, like Morandi, like
Utrillo, like Vuillard, he did not condition his age, he illumined it.
These painters are all necessary to the understanding of our time.
And Modigliani, as one of these lyricists who speak to the world
from their solitude, bore witness to his belief in the face of man
as the mirror of his own feelings ».

Franco Russoli (1959)

It pays to have another look, to observe how the artist would focus attention on a sitter's firmly defined eyes and eyebrows; on a slightly curved
nose, determined lips, a powerful chin. Or how he stressed the large forehead,
the bony structure of a face. One sitter will glance at us in a supercilious
manner; another will not look at us at all. A beggar will be painted with
deep sympathy. A person notorious for his savage and truculent personality
will be shown mercilessly with all the flaws in his mental make-up. The
artist could characterize people in the most subtle ways: by a stronger tilting
of the head, a variation of the angle of the nose, an ironical, surly or sensi-
tive mouth; the position of arms or hands; or by the deliberate application
of hot or cold pigment to provide the desired mood. His sitters often appear
as they actually were - elegant or slovenly, sensuous or dispassionate, arro-
gant or humble, intellectual or dull.

Occasionally, he could be highly critical of a person - and reveal his
disdain. On the other hand, he would lend a female sitter some of the spiritual beauty that rested in his own soul, even if she happened to be a
streetwalker, one of the simple *filles de joie* who flocked from the rural
districts to the artist's quarter in search of excitement, and were an integral
part of the scene in Montmartre and Montparnasse, Unlike Toulouse-Lautrec,
who had stressed their foul looks, their wasted bodies, Modigliani, basically
kind and warm-hearted, « improved » them on canvas (as Lunia Czechowska
put it, « Modigliani saw only that which was beautiful and pure »). Though
in his works they are not invariably pretty, they, on the other hand, evoke
our compassion. So do the neighborhood children, as yet untinged by the
sordid milieu in which they were growing up. And so do the domestics,
on their feet from daybreak till late in the evening, their chores leaving

them fatigued and untidy.

There are no « high society » portraits. With his great skill and good middleclass background Modigliani could have been even more successful as a society portraitist than another immigrant, Kees van Dongen, who earned a fortune by sticking to a formula - making women appear slimmer and their jewels fatter. Modigliani refused to market himself and his talents. Moreover, like Rembrandt, he preferred to keep company « mostly with common people and such as practised art ».

Nor is it likely that he could have made as many concessions to Realism as did the money-minded Van Dongen. The « abstract » qualities would have turned away all potential customers (there are no *nouveaux riches* among his sitters, as far as we know). This trend towards abstraction he shared with the sculptors Elie Nadelman and Constantin Brancusi, and with the anonymous African, archaic Greek and Indo-Chinese carvers. For a while, Brancusi exerted the deepest influence upon him; through the linear rhythm and relation of masses, the solidity of forms which allow no articulation of parts of the body and, finally, that simplicification which is always the mark of a good sculptor. But the Roumanian stuck to his three-dimensioned work, gradually turning from the human figure to express his vision in near-abstract shapes of seals, turtles, birds and fish. His disciple Modigliani not only abandoned sculpture for painting, but also adhered to the human motif to his end.

His humanism can be spotted even in his most « abstract » works, the caryatids (painted largely during the period when the artist was concentrating on sculpture), and the many nudes. Modigliani's nude - mostly posed seated or lying on her back - is often austere. Her body is placed against gradated areas of non-representational color, designed solely to set off the flesh tones and the dark hair. The face of this nude, as a rule, does not have the psychological complexity with which Modigliani was concerned when countenances were the primary subject of his painting. The body is generally a combination of elementary stereometric shapes - interlocking cylinders, spheres, ovoids, cones and cubes. Nonetheless, this nude is not a piece of sculpture carved out of a pinkish or yellowish stone. It is a woman with sensuous appeal, though the voluptuousness is kept under control.

Indeed, Modigliani's nudes - placed in rooms barely sketched in general terms, or radically ignored - are among the « coolest » ever painted, and yet enormously seductive to the viewer who discerns the excitement that went into these transfigurations of ordinary bodies into chromatic poems, sinuous arabesques of thin limbs and high waists. Perhaps the police official who in 1917 had the paintings removed from the show window of the Berthe Weill gallery in Paris (during Modigliani's only and hardly successful one-man show) was prompted to this action not so much by the unusual display of pubic hair as by the subconscious awareness that these unnaturalistic nudes exuded far more sexuality than the anatomically very correct nudes painted, say, by the celebrated academician Adolphe-William Bouguereau. As late as 1929, Lamberto Vitali, in compiling a book of Modigliani's drawings, felt compelled to omit some of them: « In order to avoid offending official decency or incurring the sanctions set forth in . . . the (Italian) Penal Code, I have decided not to reproduce any of the nudes that have been denounced ».

And not so many years ago, the postal authorities demanded that New York's Guggenheim Museum withdraw from sale postcards reproducing Modigliani's *Nu Couché Dormeuse*. A *Life* article on Modigliani provoked many letters of protest, one ending with this line: « Nothing prevents me from ripping the dirt from the pages of your magazine before such ' art ' inspires my children ». All these reactions simply indicate that Modigliani succeeded in filling his work with vitality and zest. Sir Kenneth Clark, in his book *The Nude,* formulates his justification when he writes: « No nude, however abstract, should fail to arouse in the spectator some vestige of erotic feeling . . . and if it does not do so, it is bad art and false morals ».

« Ethics », which distinguishes between the truly good and bad, might have been an even better word, for « morals » refers only to society's generally accepted standards. Modigliani's nudes have none of the hypocrisy of those of Bouguereau, who gave his pictures a tincture of lewdness under the cover of classical title. Modigliani had high principles as an artist and as a man. No memoir ever reports a single mean act by this most excitable and often irascible man. He loved people - and his portraits of people glow with subdued fire. Any one of his great portraits could be described as an « Arrangement of Ovoids and Cylinders ». It is this, all right, but it is also no more anti-humanistically abstract than is Whistler's portrait of his mother, though the American artist called it challengingly, an « Arrangement in Grey and Black ».

Significantly, Modigliani did not permit himself to be drawn into the Cubist movement, for which man was uninteresting except for his « geometry ». Futurism, with its hatred of the nude, and of Old Master art, was anathema to him (though the movement's originators were Italians who even tried hard to woo him). In a subtle way, Modigliani somehow succeeded in reconciling the representational and the nonrepresentational. He fulfilled the demands of the purists, who emphasized that a picture was a plane surface covered with colors in a certain order, but he also provided his canvases with rich human, sexual and social implications. He revealed and concealed, took away and added, seduced and soothed. This inspired eclectic - who was aristocratic, socialist and sensualist in one person - triumphantly combined some of the features by Ivory Coast craftsmen with those of the Byzantine and early Renaissance icon makers to shape pulsating Modiglianis!

I V

A feature that he shares with none of his contemporaries is his treatment of the eye. Quite frequently he achieved mystery by a simple device - closing the « window of the soul », or indicating the eye as just a narrow blue or brown slit. Perhaps this elision of the eye was meant to shut out the hostile world, to foster concentration upon oneself. Or perhaps the introspective artist came to feel that it was as preposterous to paint an eye as to try to render the sun.

Mademoiselle Hebuterne « looks » at us through blue slits, Miss Hastings through brown ones. Even the briefest text about the artist must mention these two, whose likenesses often appear in his oeuvre, and who moulded his life in many ways. Beatrice Hastings, a young English woman with literary talent, first met Modigliani in 1914. The two years which the artist spent with this energetic and rather eccentric person were stormy ones, but they were also most fruitful. Miss Hastings recognized his gifts at a time when few took him seriously and she tried hard to keep him out of mischief and to make him work. His portraits of Beatrice have quite angular designs: planes intersect sharply, straight lines are more dominant than curves, and there is, altogether, a precise articulation of volumes not to be found in the more lyrical portraits of Jeanne.

Obviously, this kind of pictorial treatment better suited the character of this very intellectual female who left the artist after recognizing it was beyond her power to check his wild excesses. Jeanne, a young art student, met him in 1917, bore him a daughter, and remained his steadfast companion even in death (in a state of advanced pregnancy, she committed suicide a few hours after Modigliani died). Jeanne appears as the sweet, delicate and submissive person she was. It was in the gentle features of this Botticellesque girl that Modigliani found, not only his proper model, but also his true soul-mate, the *donna che non si trova,* the « woman one never meets », and time and again he conjured up the melodious grace of her body in undulating rhythms of line and color.

Of Modigliani's personal friends who sat for him, few are still alive. One of them is the celebrated sculptor Jacques Lipchitz. In 1916, Modigliani made the now famous double portrait of Lipchitz and his wife. The price was « ten francs a sitting and a little alcohol », and the pose decided upon was one inspired by the couple's wedding photograph. As a rule, Modi finished a portrait in a few hours; this one, however, took him almost two weeks to finish. It is a good likeness, despite its freely mannerist style.

This information about the picture is derived from reminiscences Lipchitz wrote in 1951. The sculptor admired the painter, ten years his senior, not only on account of his talent, but also because of the strength of his convictions, his pride, his courage. The younger man tried to reform his friend, but it was in vain: « When I began to urge him to be less self-destructive and to put some kind of order into his life, he became more angry than I had ever seen him ».

There was solace for Lipchitz, and for all the others who were around when the painter perished miserably at the age of thirty-five: « Although he died so young, he accomplished what he wanted ». The writer made this significant addition to his biographical sketch:

« He said to me time and again that he wanted a short but intense life - *une vie brave mais intense* ».

Alfred Werner

Art historian and lecturer, Dr. Alfred Werner is the author of more than twenty books, including two on Modigliani.

CHRONOLOGY

1884   Amedeo Clemente Modigliani, born July 12 in Livorno, Italy, fourth child of Flaminio Modigliani, a small businessman, and his wife Eugenia (née Garsin). The Modiglianis and the Garsins were Sephardic Jews.

1895   Amedeo, pupil at the local *liceo* (secondary school), falls ill with pleurisy.

1898   Begins his study of drawing and painting under the guidance of Guglielmo Michele.

1901   To regain his strength after an attack of tuberculosis, he is sent on a tour of convalescence. Visits Capri, Naples and Rome.

1902   Enrolls at the Scuola Libera di Nudo of the Accademia di Bella Arti, Florence.

1903   Enrolls at the Institute di Belle Arti, Venice.

1906   Arrives in Paris in the beginning of January. Finds quarters in Montmartre.

1907   Becomes a member of the Société des Artistes Indépendents. Meets the young physician Dr. Paul Alexandre, who becomes a close friend and buys several paintings.

1908   Exhibits five paintings and a drawing at the Salon des Artistes Indépendants.

1909   Refuses to sign Futurist Manifesto. Dr. Alexandre introduces him to the sculptor Constantin Brancusi who guides his first steps in sculpture. Spends several months in Livorno.

1910   Exhibits *The Cellist* (both versions) and four other paintings at the Salon des Artistes Indépendants.

1912   Exhibits seven sculptures at the Salon d'Automne.

1914   Starts love affair with Beatrice Hastings. The poet Max Jacob introduces him to the dealer Paul Guillaume, who buys several of his pictures.

1916   Leopold Zborowski becomes his dealer.

1917   Falls in love with the art student, Jeanne Hébuterne. Oneman show at the Galerie Berthe Weill. The police order the five pictures of nudes to be removed.

1918   Stays at Cagnes on the Riviera, trying to regain his health. Meets the aged Auguste Renoir. On November 29, Jeanne Hébuterne bears him a daughter, also named Jeanne.

1919   Several of his works are included in a London group show of contemporary French art.

1920   Modigliani dies at the Hopital de la Charite on January 24. On January 25, Jeanne Hébuterne commits suicide. The artist's funeral, on January 27, at the Pere Lachaise cemetery, is attended by a large crowd of mourners.

1923   Jeanne's remains are interred with his at the cemetery, where a granite stone, with a touching inscription, now covers both graves.

1. PORTRAIT DE PEDRO 1908

2. L'AMAZONE 1909

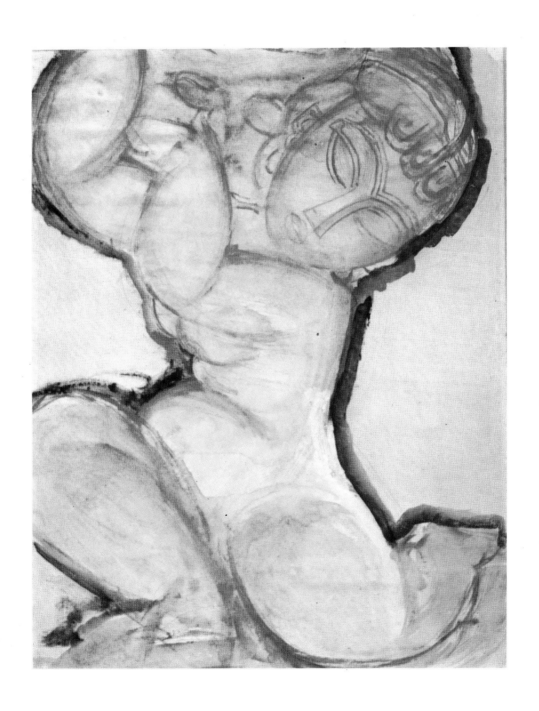

3. CARYATIDE ROSE c. 1914

4. PORTRAIT DE FRANK BURTY HAVILAND c. 1914

5. PORTRAIT DE MOISE KISLING 1915

6. PORTRAIT DE HENRI LAURENS 1915

7.   LA FANTESCA 1915

8. BEATRICE HASTINGS 1915

10.   LES MARIES 1915 - 1916

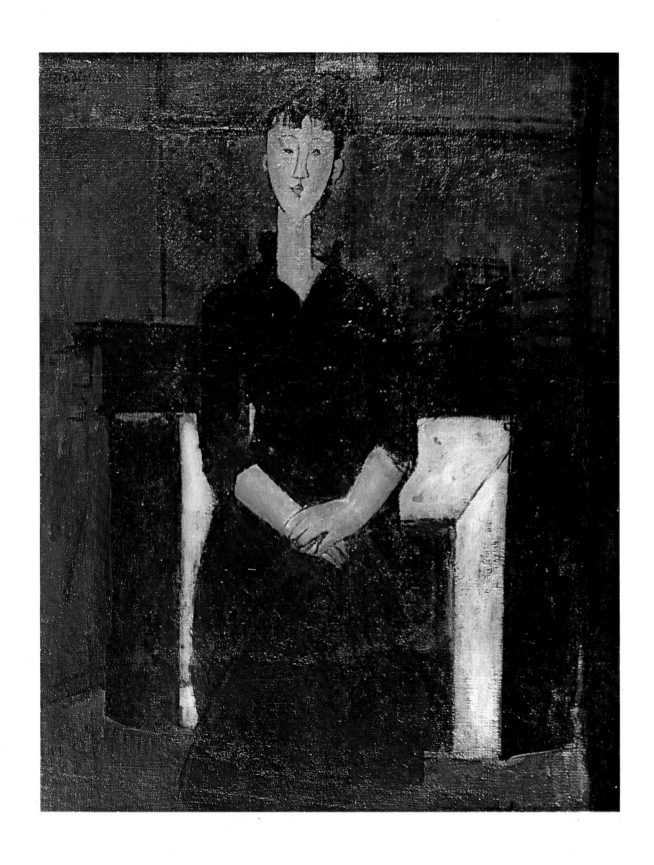

11.   DAME ASSISE DEVANT UNE CHEMINEE 1916

12. JEAN COCTEAU 1916

13.   RAIMONDE c. 1916

14. MARGUERITE 1916

15. NU AU DIVAN 1916

16.   PORTRAIT DE HANKA ZBOROWSKA 1916

17.   ELENA 1917

18. NU COUCHE AUX BRAS LEVES 1917

19. ELENA 1917

20. PORTRAIT DE LEOPOLD ZBOROWSKI 1917

21. FILLETTE ASSISE (HUGUETTE) 1917 - 1918

22.   MADAME HEBUTERNE A LA CLOCHE 1917

23.   LE GARCON ROUGE 1917

24.　NU COUCHE AUX BRAS LEVES 1917

25. HARICOT ROUGE 1917

26. PORTRAIT DE JEUNE FILLE 1917

27. LE BEAU MAJOR (DR. DEVARAIGNE) 1917

28.   NU COUCHE AU COUSSIN BLEU 1917 - 1918

29.   TETE DE FILLE c. 1917

30.   ALMAISA 1917

31. JEUNE FILLE AUX YEUX BLEUS 1917

32.   PORTRAIT DE FEMME AU CORSAGE BLEU 1917

33.   JEUNE FILLE ASSISE EN CHEMISE 1918

34.   PORTRAIT DE MADAME SURVAGE 1918

35.   PORTRAIT DE L'ACTEUR GASTON MODOT 1918

36. PORTRAIT DE FEMME AU COL BLANC 1918

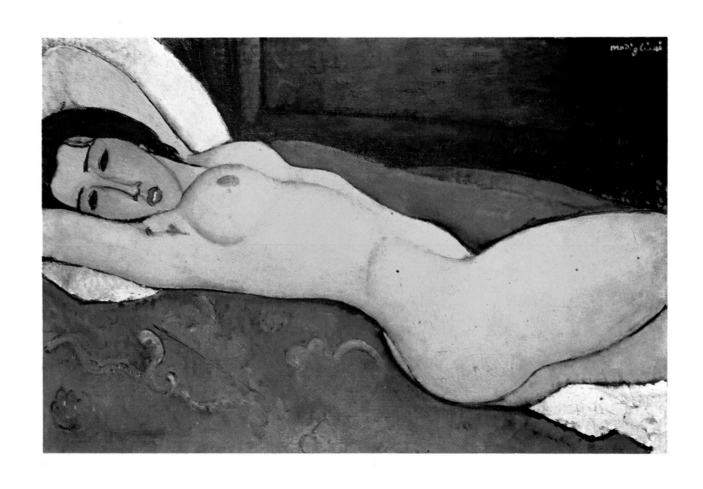

37. NU COUCHE 1918

38.   PORTRAIT DE FEMME 1918

39.   PORTRAIT DE JEUNE FILLE c. 1918

40. GARCON A LA VESTE BLEUE 1918

41. GARCON A LA VESTE BLEUE c. 1918

42.   MADAME HEBUTERNE 1918

43.   PORTRAIT DE FILLETTE 1918

44.   LA JEUNE BONNE 1919

45. PAYSAGE DU MIDI 1919

46. LA ROBE NOIRE 1919

47.   PORTRAIT DE MADAME HEBUTERNE 1919

48.   LE GRAND NU c. 1919

49.   LUNIA CZECHOWSKA 1919

50. LA FILLE DU PEUPLE 1919

52.   PORTRAIT DE THORA KLINCKOWSTROM 1919

CATALOGUE

1. PORTRAIT DE PEDRO, 1908
Oil, 21 5/8 × 18 inches
*Collection: The Freddy and
Regina T. Homburger Collection,
Housed at the Maine State
Museum, Augusta, Maine*

2. L'AMAZONE, 1909
Oil, 36 1/4 × 25 5/8 inches
*Collection: Mr. and Mrs.
Alexander Lewyt*

3. CARYATIDE ROSE, c. 1914
Gouache, 21 7/8 × 17 3/4
inches
*Collection: Mr. and Mrs.
Klaus G. Perls*

4. PORTRAIT DE FRANK
BURTY HAVILAND, c. 1914
Oil on cardboard,
24 1/2 × 19 1/2 inches
*Collection: The Los Angeles
County Museum of Art,
Mr. and Mrs. William Preston
Harrison Collection*

5. PORTRAIT DE MOISE
KISLING, 1915
Oil, 41 × 29 1/2 inches
*Collection:
Mr. Leo M. Rogers*

6. PORTRAIT DE HENRI
LAURENS, 1915
Oil, 45 3/4 × 35 inches
*Collection: Mr. and Mrs.
Robert J. Newman*

7. LA FANTESCA, 1915
Oil, 31 × 18 1/8 inches
Lent Anonymously

8. BEATRICE HASTINGS, 1915
Oil, 31 × 18 inches
*Collection:
The Ritter Foundation Inc.*

*9. LEON INDENBAUM, 1915
Oil, 21 5/8 × 17 3/4 inches
*Collection: Mr. and Mrs.
Henry Pearlman*

10. LES MARIES, 1915 - 1916
Oil, 21 3/4 × 18 1/4 inches
*Collection: The Museum of
Modern Art, New York Gift of
Frederic Clay Bartlett, 1942*

11. DAME ASSISE DEVANT
UNE CHEMINEE, 1916
Oil, 31 3/4 × 25 1/4 inches
Lent Anonymously

12. JEAN COCTEAU, 1916
Oil, 39 1/2 × 32 inches
*Collection: Mr. and Mrs.
Henry Pearlman*

13. RAIMONDE, c. 1916
Oil on board,
20 1/4 × 13 inches
James W. Alsdorf

14. MARGUERITE, 1916
Oil, 31 1/2 × 17 1/2 inches
*Collection: The Harry
N. Abrams Family Collection*

15. NU AU DIVAN, 1916
Oil, 31 7/8 × 45 5/8 inches
Collection:
Paul and Odette Wurzburger

16. PORTRAIT DE HANKA
ZBOROWSKA, 1916
Oil, 32 × 20 1/8 inches
Collection: The Alex Hillman
Family Foundation

17. ELENA, 1917
Oil, 18 1/4 × 13 inches
Collection:
Mr. Edward A. Bragaline

18. NU COUCHE AUX BRAS
LEVES, 1917
Oil, 23 5/8 × 36 1/4 inches
Collection :
Mrs. Evelyn Sharp

19. ELENA, 1917
Oil, 25 1/2 × 19 1/4 inches
Collection:
The Phillips Collection

20. PORTRAIT DE LEOPOLD
ZBOROWSKI, 1917
Oil, 45 3/4 × 28 3/4 inches
Collection:
Mr. and Mrs. John A. Beck

21. FILLETTE ASSISE
(HUGUETTE), 1917 - 1918
Oil, 36 × 23 3/4 inches
Lent Anonymously

22. MADAME HEBUTERNE
A LA CLOCHE, 1917
Oil, 28 1/2 × 23 inches
Collection:
Mr. Edward A. Bragaline

23. LE GARCON ROUGE, 1917
Oil, 36 × 23 1/2 inches
Collection:
Mrs. Evelyn Sharp

24. NU COUCHE AUX BRAS
LEVES, 1917
Oil, 25 1/2 × 39 3/8 inches
Collection:
Mr. Richard S. Zeisler

25. HARICOT ROUGE, 1917
Oil, 21 5/8 × 15 inches
Collection:
Mr. and Mrs. Arnold Askin

26. PORTRAIT DE JEUNE
FILLE, 1917
Oil, 23 3/4 × 18 1/4 inches
Collection: The Metropolitan
Museum of Art, New York
Gift of Charles F. Iklé, 1960

27. LE BEAU MAJOR
(DR. DEVARAIGNE), 1917
Oil, 21 3/4 × 18 inches
Collection:
The Evergreen House, Baltimore

28. NU COUCHE AU COUSSIN
BLEU, 1917 - 1918
Oil, 25 1/2 × 39 1/2 inches
Collection:
Mr. Nathan Cummings

29. TETE DE FILLE, c. 1917
Oil, 25 1/2 × 18 inches
Collection:
Mr. Joseph H. Hazen

30. ALMAISA, 1917
Oil, 36 1/4 × 21 1/4 inches
Lent Anonymously

31. JEUNE FILLE AUX YEUX
BLEUS, 1917
Oil, 24 × 18 1/4 inches
Collection: The Marion Koogler
McNay Art Institute,
San Antonio

32. PORTRAIT DE FEMME
AU CORSAGE BLEU, 1917
Oil, 24 × 18 1/8 inches
Lent Anonymously

33. JEUNE FILLE ASSISE EN
CHEMISE, 1918
Oil, 31 7/8 × 21 1/4 inches
Collection:
Mr. and Mrs. Keith Barish

34. PORTRAIT DE MADAME
SURVAGE, 1918
Oil, 17 1/4 × 11 inches
Collection:
Mr. and Mrs. Gustave Ring

35. PORTRAIT DE L'ACTEUR
GASTON MODOT, 1918
Oil, 18 1/8 × 13 inches
Collection:
Mr. and Mrs. Simon Jaglom

36. PORTRAIT DE FEMME
AU COL BLANC, 1918
Oil, 24 1/2 × 17 3/4 inches
Lent Anonymously

37. NU COUCHE, 1918
Oil, 23 5/8 × 36 1/4 inches
Collection:
Mr. and Mrs. Klaus G. Perls

38. PORTRAIT DE FEMME, 1918
Oil, 24 1/2 × 17 1/2 inches
Collection:
Mr. R. Sturgis Ingersoll

39. PORTRAIT JEUNE FILLE,
c. 1918
Oil, 24 × 15 inches
Lent Anonymously

40. GARCON A LA VESTE
BLEUE, 1918
Oil, 36 1/2 × 24 1/4 inches
Collection: The Solomon
R. Guggenheim Museum,
New York

41. GARCON A LA VESTE
BLEUE, c. 1918
Oil, 36 1/4 × 23 3/4 inches
Collection:
The Indianapolis Museum of Art
Gift of Mrs. Julian Bobbs
in Memory
of William Ray Adams

42. MADAME HEBUTERNE, 1918
Oil, 36 /4 × 21 1/4 inches
Collection: Katherine and the
Late Adolphe A. Juviler

43. PORTRAIT DE FILLETTE, 1918
Oil, 23 5/8 × 19 3/4 inches
Collection:
Mr. and Mrs. Paul Sampliner

44. LA JEUNE BONNE, 1919
Oil, 60 × 24 inches
Collection: Albright-Knox
Art Gallery, Buffalo

45. PAYSAGE DU MIDI, 1919
Oil, 23 5/8 × 17 3/4 inches
Lent Anonymously

46. LA ROBE NOIRE, 1919
Oil, 37 × 23 1/2 inches
Lent Anonymously

47. PORTRAIT DE MADAME HEBUTERNE, 1919
Oil, 39 3/8 × 25 1/2 inches
Collection: The Solomon R.
Guggenheim Museum, New York

48. LE GRAND NU, c. 1919
Oil, 28 1/2 × 45 7/8 inches
Collection: The Museum of
Modern Art, New York Mrs.
Simon Guggenheim Fund, 1950

49. LUNIA CZECHOWSKA, 1919
Oil, 18 1/2 × 13 inches
Lent Anonymously

50. LA FILLE DU PEUPLE, 1919
Oil, 39 1/4 × 25 1/4 inches
Collection: The Los Angeles
County Museum of Art, Gift of
Dr. and Mrs. Armand Hammer

*51. JEANNE HEBUTERNE ASSISE DEVANT UN LIT, 1919
Oil, 21 3/ 4 × 15 inches
Lent Anonymously

52. PORTRAIT DE THORA KLINCKOWSTROM, 1919
Oil, 38 × 25 inches
Lent Anonymously

* Works marked with an asterisk unfortunately are not illustrated in the catalogue as photographs were not available at the time of printing.

SELECTED BIBLIOGRAPHY

BASLER, Adolphe, *Modigliani*, Paris, Crès, 1931

BERTRAM, Anthony, *Amedeo Modigliani*, London

BORCHERT, Bernhart, *Modigliani*, London, Faber & Faber, c. 1960

CARCO, Francis, *De Montmartre au Quartier Latin*, Paris, Michel, 1927

CARRIERI, Raffaele, *Dodici Opere di Amedeo Modigliani*, Milan, Edizione del Milione, 1947

CERONI, Ambrogio, *Modigliani, peintre*, Milan, Edizione del Milione, 1958

CERONI, Ambrogio, *Modigliani, dessins et sculptures*, Milan, Edizione del Milione, 1965

COCTEAU, Jean, *Modigliani*, Paris, Hazan, 1950

DALE, Maud, *Modigliani*, New York, A.A. Knopf, 1929

DESCARGUES, Pierre, *Modigliani*, Paris, Braun, 1951

DIEHL, Gaston, *Modigliani*, New York, 1969

DOUGLAS, Charles, *Artist Quarter*, London, Faber & Faber, 1941

FRANCHI, Raffaele, *Modigliani*, 3rd edition, Florence, Arnaud, 1946

JEDLICKA, Gottfried, *Modigliani*, Zurich, Eugen Reutsch, 1953

LANTHEMANN, Joseph, *Catalogue raisonné de l'oeuvre de Modigliani*, Montreux, Editions Jornod, 1970

LIPCHITZ, Jacques, and WERNER, Alfred, *Modigliani*, New York, 1970

MODESTI, Renzo, *Modigliani*, Milan, Vallardi, 1959

MODIGLIANI, Jeanne, *Modigliani: Man and Myth*, New York, Orion, 1958

PAVOLINI, Corrado, *Modigliani*, Milan, 1966

PICCIONI, Leone and CERONI, Ambrogio, *I dipinti di Modigliani*, Milan, Rizzoli, 1970

PFANNSTIEL, Arthur, *Modigliani, L'art et la vie*, Paris, Marcel Scheur, 1929

PFANNSTIEL, Arthur, *Modigliani et son oeuvre*, Paris, 1956

RAYNAL, Maurice, *Modigliani*, Geneva, Paris and New York, Skira, 1951

ROY, Claude, *Modigliani*, Geneve, Skira, 1958

RUSSOLI, Franco, *Modigliani*, New York, 1959

RUSSOLI, Franco, *Modigliani: Drawings and Sketches*, New York, 1969

SALMON, André, *Modigliani, sa vie et son oeuvre*, Paris, 1926

SALMON, André, *La Vie passionée de Modigliani*, Paris, 1957

SAN LAZZARO, Giorgio di, *Modigliani peintures*, Paris, Editions de Chene, 1953

SCHAUB-KOCH, Emile, *Amedeo Modigliani*, Paris and Lille, Mercure Universal, 1933

SCHEIWILLER, Giovanni, editor, *Omaggio a Modigliani*, Milan, Hoepli, 1930

SCHEIWILLER, Giovanni, *Amedeo Modigliani*, 5th edition, Milan, 1950

SCHEIWILLER, Giovanni, *Modigliani*, Zurich, 1958

SICHEL, Pierre, *Modigliani*, New York, 1967

SOBI, James Thrall, *Modigliani*, New York, 1951

VITALI, Lamberto, *Disegni di Modigliani*, Milan, Hoepli, 1929

VLAMINCK, Maurice, *Tournant Dangereux*, London, 1961

WERNER, Alfred, *Modigliani the Sculptor*, New York, 1962

WERNER, Alfred, *Modigliani*, New York, Harry Abrams, 1966